IN AFRICA

Marc & Evelyne Bernheim

A MARGARET K. MCELDERRY BOOK

IN AFRICA

Atheneum   1974   New York

In Africa

you will find jungles,

3

deserts,

FOR LYNN

Copyright © 1973 by Marc & Evelyne Bernheim. All rights reserved. Library of Congress catalog card number 72-85913. ISBN 0-689-30315-7
Published simultaneously in Canada by McClelland & Stewart, Ltd. Manufactured in the United States of America. Printed by The Murray Printing Company, Forge Village, Massachusetts. Bound by A. Horowitz & Son/Bookbinders, Clifton, New Jersey. With grateful acknowledgement to Earle Kersh for the layout of the book. First Printing February 1973. Second Printing February 1974.

4

mountains,

rivers,

great plains,

and cities,
lots of new
cities.

You will see all sorts of houses:

some square,

some round,

some very tall.

some very low,

There are houses on stilts

and houses you can climb in and out of

to visit friends on rooftops.

What sort of people live in those houses?

They don't look alike. They don't dress alike.

17

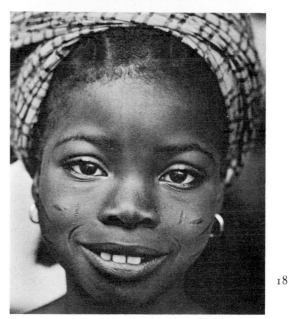

18

Sometimes their clothes 16

or the marks on their faces
can tell you where
they come from.

What do people do?

Some are cattlemen,

or policewomen,

20

19

miners,

21

or airline hostesses,

22

23   farmers,   24   drummers,

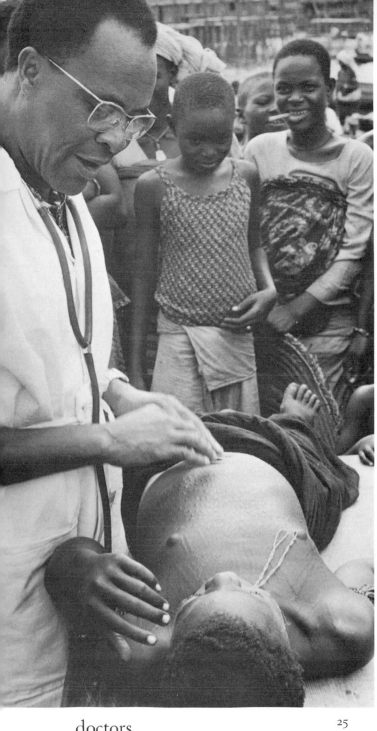

doctors,

kings.

25   26

If you live
in the savanna,

27

28

where the tall grass grows,

your home may be a hut

with a straw roof

that needs changing every year.

Your father is a farmer
growing yams or cotton.

Your mother walks to market.
She carries food to sell in a basin.

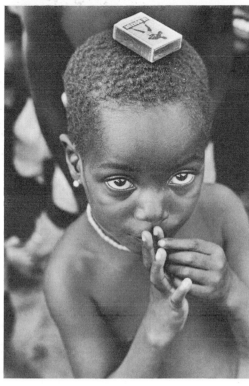

From her you learn
to balance things
on your head.

When you go to school,
you bring your own seat.

In the afternoon,
you go with friends
to pick cotton in the fields.

Most of your life
takes place outside.
Here your mother
washes the baby
and cooks.

37

Inside is for chickens,

38

for listening to the radio,

and for sleeping.

39

If you live
in the forest,

your village may be small.

All your family lives together.

43

While you are in school,
your mother, sister, and aunts
pound yams for lunch.

44

When father returns from the forest,
the boys eat with him.

45

You play African checkers,

you dive into the river,

46

47

you make your own scooter out of wood,

wheels and all.

Sometimes you can
hear elephants,
or big machines
cutting and
loading trees,

or the tap-tap of
Grandfather's tool,
as he carves a mask
you wear for dancing.

50

52

51

One day he will show you
the little gods who protect
the forest where you live.

If you live
in the desert,

you are always on the move.

and are a nomad boy,

When you find a water well, you stop.

You unpack your tent.
This is home for a while.

57

Your father wears a veil
to protect him
from sand storms.

You help take care of the camels,

58

60

Your mother wears
make-up for holidays.

and on holidays you race on them.

Your camel may not look beautiful,

but he is your best friend

because he takes you places.

When there is no more grass
for the camels to eat,
Mother starts folding the tent.
You go to buy food at a faraway market and move again.

You see new things
when you travel:
men building a railroad,
trucks and planes
crossing the desert,

and, if you travel far enough, you can find temples built long ago when the land was green.

If you live
on the coast,

your village may look like this.
Your father is a fisherman.

70

Grandfather is too old to go fishing.

He watches the men get the boats ready.

It is very dangerous to go through the big waves.

72

When the boats return, everyone pulls the net.

Sometimes there are hardly any fish.

Then the men walk back home in silence.

If you catch a lot of fish,
your family sells them in the city.

Your school can be a hut in the sand.

If you are small enough,
you will ride to market
on your brother's back.

Sundays are for wrestling,

for drumming,

or for quiet walks in the sand.

If you live
in the city,

your house may be here.

84

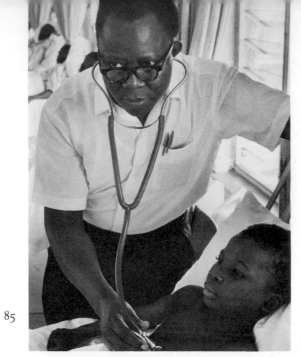

85

Your father may be a doctor.

86

Your mother may sell cloth
at the market.

In the city there are too many people, too many cars.

87

You can play traffic
jam with cars
you make out of wire.

You can go to the zoo,

or to the airport and watch the planes.

But best of all, you can have all these friends: they
come from the savanna, the forest, the desert, or the
coast, and that's what life in Africa is like.

Captions for Photographs

In Africa there are many more geographical regions than the five shown here. Each section in this book is made up of photographs taken in many different countries. The following list of captions shows where in Africa each photograph was taken:

1) *Kenya:* giraffes, Mara reserve 2) *Ivory Coast:* rain forest 3) *Mauretania:* water well near Aroit 4) *Ethiopia:* landscape with farms near Harrar 5) *Cameroun:* fishermen in Logone River 6) *Tanzania:* wildebeests and car at N'Gorongoro crater 7) *Nigeria:* Lagos, the capital 8) *Ivory Coast:* Senufo huts near Sinématiali 9) *Ivory Coast:* apartments in Abidjan 10) *Niger Republic:* Tuareg tent near Tillabéry 11) *Nigeria:* a Lagos building with statue of Shango, Yoruba god of thunder 12) *Dahomey:* stilt houses at Ganvié 13) *Ghana:* boys climb "ladder" to go out of compound. Nayagnia village, North Ghana 14) *Ghana:* Nayagnia village houses, Kassem group 15) *Ghana:* Accra policeman and pedestrians 16) *Kenya:* Morani Masai warriors, Kajiado region 17) *Togo:* Fulani girl with paint make-up, at Lama-Kara 18) *Nigeria:* little Yoruba girl near Ibadan 19) *Niger Republic:* Fulani cattleman near Agadès 20) *Guinea:* Policewoman training in Conakry 21) *South Africa:* gold miner near Johannesburg 22) *Nigeria:* Nigeria Airways hostess at Lagos Airport 23) *Sudan:* cotton farmer, Gezira scheme 24) *Ghana:* Nayagnia village drummer, Kassem group 25) *Dahomey:* Dr. Akouete and patient, Ganvié village 26) *Nigeria:* the king of Akure, West Nigeria

SAVANNA

27) *Ivory Coast:* Hausa girl, Sinématiali area 28) *Togo:* one-family hut compound in the Cabrais region 29) *Nigeria:* farmer carries straw-thatched roof to his hut. Near Katsina 30) *Togo:* farmer and yam mounds, Cabrais region 31) *Nigeria:* Fulani women going to market, near Kaduna 32) *Ivory Coast:* little girl carrying matchbox on head, at Bingerville 33) *Ivory Coast:* schoolchildren from Konamoukro village, Baoule group 34) *Zambia:* children going to the field, near Mansa 35) *Ivory Coast:* mother washing baby, Dan region, northwest Ivory Coast 36) *Zambia:* cooking scene in compound near Monze, Tonga group 37) *Zambia:* women and chickens in hut near Mansa 38) *Zambia:* listening to radio in hut, near Mansa 39) *Zambia:* sleeping in hut near Monze, Tonga group

FOREST

40) *Nigeria:* Yoruba drummer boy, near Ogbomosho 41) *Liberia:* forest village near Zorzor 42) *Ivory Coast:* cocoa farmer's family at Yaou, Abouré group 43) *Ivory Coast:* women pounding yams, Yaou village 44) *Ivory Coast:* father eating *foufou* with children, Yaou village 45) *Ivory Coast:* boys playing checkers, Yaou village 46) *Ivory Coast:* boy diving into river, Yaou village. 47) *Cameroun:* boys riding homemade wood bicycles, near Bangagté. 48) *Tanzania:* elephants at Lake Manyara 49) *Nigeria:* logging in the Calabar forest 50) *Ivory Coast:* Dan carver and grandson at Gangouin village 51) *Ivory Coast:* Dan boy trying on mask, Gangouin village 52) *Nigeria:* Ibo clay figures, Anni shrine, Enugu region

DESERT

53) *Niger Republic:* nomad Tuareg boy near Agadès 54) *Niger Republic:* Tuareg nomad caravan near Agadès 55) *Niger Republic:* Tuareg nomads and herd at well near Agadès 56) *Niger Republic:* Tuareg nomad tent near Abalak. Woman playing the *amzad* violin 57) *Niger Republic:* Tuareg nomad at Ayourou 58) *Niger Republic:* Tuareg nomad woman near Tahoua 59) *Niger Republic:* camels drinking at Abalak pumping station 60) *Niger Republic:* boys racing on camels, near Abalak 61) *Ethiopia:* close-up of camel chewing leaves 62) *Ethiopia:* close-up of camel chewing leaves 63) *Ethiopia:* close-up of camel chewing leaves 64) *Niger Republic:* Tuareg woman folding up tent, near Abalak 65) *Niger Republic:* Barmou market and Hausa huts 66) *Mauretania:* nomads building railroad at Fort Gouraud 67) *Sudan:* pyramids at Meroë.

COAST:

68) *Togo:* little girl with brother, near Lomé 69) *Ivory Coast:* fishing village near Abidjan 70) *Ghana:* old man looking at Old Jamestown fishing harbor, Accra 71) *Dahomey:* fishing canoe out at sea, near Cotonou 72) *Ivory Coast:* pulling in net, near Abidjan 73) *Ivory Coast:* little boys and fish, near Abidjan 74) *Togo:* Ewe fishermen carrying nets home, near Lomé 75) *Ivory Coast:* Abidjan fish auction 76) *Togo:* Ewe schoolchildren at Akodessewa village 77) *Ivory Coast:* little girl tying up baby brother on brother's back, Yaou village 78) *Dahomey:* Cotonou market 79) *Senegal:* Senegalese wrestling match 80) *Ghana:* Akosombo drummers 81) *Ivory Coast:* family walks in the sand, near Bingerville.

CITY:

82) *Nigeria:* little Yoruba girl, Lagos 83) *Nigeria:* area of Surulers housing, in a Lagos suburb 84) *Nigeria:* ice-cream man and children in Surulere housing, Lagos 85) *Nigeria:* Dr. Ogunlesi making his rounds at University College Hospital, Ibadan 86) *Togo:* Mme. Euniké Adabunu, cloth vendor, Lomé 87) *Nigeria:* traffic on Carter Bridge, Lagos 88) *Zambia:* boys with homemade wire cars, Chingola mining town 89) *Ivory Coast:* schoolchildren and giraffe at Abidjan zoo 90) *Ivory Coast:* Abidjan airport 91) *Dahomey:* cheering schoolchildren of Abomey.